Americana

ROCK 'N' ROLL
THEN AND NOW

Abdo & Daughters
MIDDLE GRADE NONFICTION

An Imprint of Abdo Publishing
abdobooks.com

R.L. Van

ABDOBOOKS.COM

Published by Abdo Publishing, a division of ABDO, PO Box 398166, Minneapolis, Minnesota 55439.

Printed in the United States of America, North Mankato, Minnesota

102023

012024

THIS BOOK CONTAINS RECYCLED MATERIALS

Design: Kelly Doudna, Mighty Media, Inc.

Production: Denise Hamernik, Mighty Media, Inc.

Editor: Liz Salzmann

Cover Photographs: Getty Images (both)

Interior Photographs: Alamy Stock Photo, p. 17; AP Images, pp. 28, 34–35; Flickr, pp. 8–9, 20, 21; Getty Images, p. 1 (both); Mighty Media, Inc., pp. 42–43; Shutterstock Images, pp. 7, 11, 14–15, 26, 33, 38, 39, 40, 41, 45 (bottom); Wikimedia Commons, pp. 3, 4–5, 10, 12, 13, 16, 18, 19, 22, 24–25, 27, 29, 30, 31, 32, 36, 37, 44, 45 (top)

Design Elements: iStockphoto

LIBRARY OF CONGRESS CONTROL NUMBER: 2023939342

PUBLISHER'S CATALOGING-IN-PUBLICATION DATA

Names: Van, R.L., author.

Title: Rock 'n' roll: then and now / by R.L. Van

Other title: then and now

Description: Minneapolis, Minnesota : Abdo Publishing, 2024 | Series: Americana | Includes online resources and index.

Identifiers: ISBN 9781098291778 (lib. bdg.) | ISBN 9781098278670 (ebook)

Subjects: LCSH: Americana--Juvenile literature. | Rock music--Juvenile literature. | Music--History and criticism--Juvenile literature. | History, Modern--Juvenile literature.

Classification: DDC 973.0--dc23

TABLE OF CONTENTS

By the end of 1964, two Beatles songs, "I Want to Hold Your Hand" and "She Loves You," were at the top of the US *Billboard* Hot 100.

Chapter 1

BEATLEMANIA COMES TO AMERICA

Families gather around their television sets. It's February 9, 1964, a Sunday night. *The Ed Sullivan Show* will be starting soon. People across the country often tune into the variety show to see exciting performances, but tonight is special. The Beatles will perform live for the first time on American television. The British band's music has been playing on the radio for weeks. Now, fans will finally see the band that has captivated the nation.

Ed Sullivan, the show's host, introduces the Beatles. Then the camera shows the Beatles onstage. They wear matching suits and their signature mop-top haircuts. The band starts playing "All My Loving." The studio audience screams throughout the performance.

More than 70 million households tune in to see the Beatles' debut on *The Ed Sullivan Show*. This is even more than the 60 million that watched Elvis Presley's debut on the show eight years earlier. In fact, it's more than one-third of the entire US population. It is a new record to mark a historic moment in American rock 'n' roll history: the British Invasion has begun.

What Is Rock 'n' Roll?

Rock 'n' roll dates back to the 1950s and has certain recognizable traits. The songs are energetic, with a fast beat and a driving rhythm. They feature drum kits and electric instruments, especially the electric guitar. They have catchy refrains. Rock lyrics can be about anything, but early lyrics were often about the experiences and dreams of teenagers. Humorous lyrics also appealed to rock's young audience. Artists still produce rock music today, but when people think of "rock 'n' roll," they are typically thinking of music from the 1950s and 1960s.

Rock 'n' Roll Then and Now

Rock 'n' roll has been a big part of American life for many decades. It has deep roots in US history and culture. From the early music that influenced and developed into rock 'n' roll, through the British Invasion, to today's rock music, rock 'n' roll has continued to evolve.

Over the years, American culture helped to both create and change rock 'n' roll music. At the same time, this music played a major role in influencing other parts of American life and culture. While musicians in many countries create rock music, rock 'n' roll will always be associated with American music and life.

The invention of the electric guitar, amplifier, and microphone played a big role in the development of rock 'n' roll music.

Jazz singer Big Joe Turner was a rock 'n' roll pioneer. In the 1930s and 1940s, he sang many jazz songs that had rock 'n' roll elements.

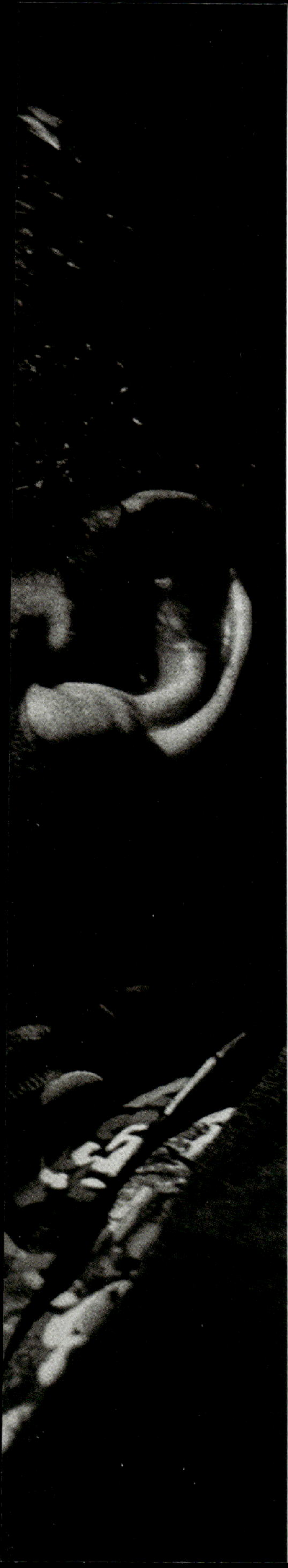

Chapter 2

ROCKING ROOTS

Rock 'n' roll has been around for less than a century. But it has a unique and exciting history. A mix of many different music genres led to the birth of rock 'n' roll. Many of rock 'n' roll's influences were rooted in Black American culture. The genre became established as its own style of music in the 1950s. As the music spread, rock 'n' roll was beloved by young people across the country.

A Genre Is Born

Rock 'n' roll was influenced by many types of music, including gospel, jazz, and country. But the biggest influence on rock 'n' roll was rhythm and blues music, or R&B. R&B was developed by Black Americans in the 1940s. It grew from the blues, which was created by Black Americans in the South after slavery ended.

R&B was popular among Black Americans throughout the 1940s, especially in big cities. But in April 1951, an R&B song called "Rocket 88" was released. The song was recorded by the band

Ike Turner and His Kings of Rhythm. Jackie Brenston was usually the band's saxophonist, but he sang the vocals for "Rocket 88." A mix-up at the studio led to the song being officially credited to Jackie Brenston and His Delta Cats. "Rocket 88" was different from other R&B songs. It had a faster tempo, distorted electric guitar, and a driving rhythm. These and other elements led many experts to later identify it as the first rock 'n' roll song.

Ike Turner (*right*) later became well-known for the music he recorded with his wife Tina Turner (*left*) in the 1960s and 1970s.

Transforming R&B

Beyond the pioneering "Rocket 88," many other Black artists added new sounds to R&B. These elements helped create rock 'n' roll. For example, Little Richard was an important artist in the creation of rock 'n' roll in the 1950s. His use of piano, exclamations, and a unique vocal style were major influences on the genre. He also had a wild stage presence and crossed gender boundaries. Little Richard's rebellious attitude was part of the spirit of rock 'n' roll, and he inspired artists for decades to come.

Chuck Berry was another important influence on rock 'n' roll. His guitar playing put the electric guitar in the spotlight for the first time. He made up cool rock 'n' roll dance moves. He wrote lyrics that focused on teen experiences and on racial issues in the country. His song "Johnny B. Goode" was the only rock song included by the National Aeronautics and Space Administration in a collection of songs sent out to space to represent music on Earth.

Little Richard received many awards and honors for his music. These included being inducted into the Rock and Roll Hall of Fame and the Songwriters Hall of Fame.

Fats Domino, Bo Diddley, and Sister Rosetta Tharpe were other major artists credited with influencing rock 'n' roll. Fats Domino's piano rhythms influenced the feel of rock 'n' roll music. Bo Diddley is known for being one of the first to use his guitar to create a beat rather than a melody or an accompaniment. Sister Rosetta Tharpe was a gospel singer whose distorted electric guitar and combination of musical styles directly influenced many rock 'n' roll stars.

Many other Black artists and groups brought innovations that became important aspects of rock 'n' roll. These innovations included a cappella groups, a rhythmic vocal style, girl groups, and more. The world of rock 'n' roll would not exist without the innovative music of Black Americans.

Sister Rosetta Tharpe is often called "the Godmother of Rock 'n' Roll."

Chuck Berry was inducted into the Rock and Roll Hall of Fame in 1986.

Ray Charles was a popular R&B artist in the 1950s. He was also one of the first Black musicians to be given artistic control over his music by a major record company.

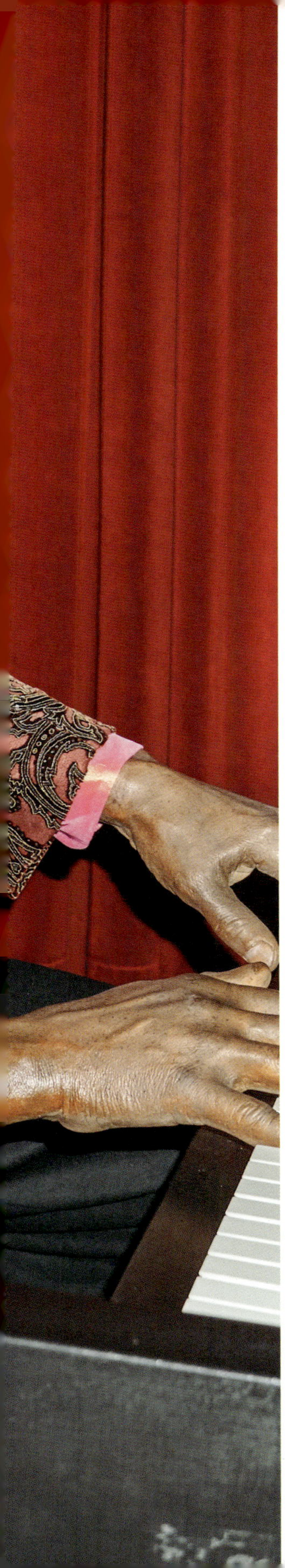

Chapter 3

A NEW ERA

The new style of R&B music popularized by Black artists began to gain popularity across the country. Young listeners loved the high-energy, dance-worthy beats. The music industry picked up on the genre's popularity. White artists began to rise to rock 'n' roll fame, often at the expense of the Black artists who created the genre. Though its history is complicated, it's undeniable that rock 'n' roll was a defining influence on the 1950s.

Name of the Game

In July 1951, a disc jockey (DJ) named Alan Freed started a radio show for R&B songs. He called it *Moondog's Rock and Roll Party*. He played R&B songs such as "Rocket 88" that are now considered to have rock 'n' roll characteristics. Freed would shout "Rock and roll!" on the show, and he called the songs he played rock 'n' roll songs.

The term *rock 'n' roll* existed long before Freed's show. It was used in the 1922 song "My Baby Rocks

Me with One Steady Roll" by Trixie Smith. And it had been used by Black Americans for many years to refer to sex. But Freed turned the term *rock 'n' roll* into a way to refer to the music genre. He also played an important role in popularizing the genre itself.

Alan Freed became famous in the United States and Europe for playing R&B music and using the term *rock 'n' roll*.

Whitewashing Black Music

American culture in the 1950s affected the way Black rock 'n' roll stars were perceived. Segregation was common across the country, although laws were starting to change. R&B was considered Black music. Its audiences were mostly Black. But thanks to radio DJs like Alan Freed, white audiences began listening to R&B music with rock 'n' roll elements. Both Black and white teenagers loved the sound.

However, racism often prevented Black rock 'n' roll artists from seeing the success they deserved. Due to segregation and racism, Black artists had to worry about their safety while performing and were sometimes unable to give concerts for white audiences. In part because of racist attitudes toward the genre's roots, white adults often believed rock 'n' roll was immoral. They tried to prevent young people from listening to it, especially when it was recorded by Black musicians. Some radio stations wouldn't play rock 'n' roll by Black artists, and many major record labels didn't want to record Black rock 'n' roll music.

The Kingsmen was a group of white artists that recorded a popular version of Black artist Richard Berry's song "Louie Louie" in 1963.

White music professionals decided to make money off rock 'n' roll by having white artists perform their own versions of Black artists' songs. Sometimes they would change the song to make it appeal more to white audiences. More often, they just had artists cover the song almost exactly as the original artist had recorded it.

This was unfair to Black artists. People purchased the records by white artists instead of the originals by Black performers. The white performers were sometimes given writing credits even though they didn't help write the songs. This meant the original Black artists weren't paid as much as they should have been for their work.

Buddy Holly was inspired to pursue his music career by Elvis Presley. He started out performing country-and-western music. But after opening for Presley a few times, Holly switched to rock 'n' roll.

"The King of Rock 'n' Roll"

White artists didn't only cover Black songs. Many white rock 'n' roll artists made their own music. And some had a big impact on rock 'n' roll. For example, Buddy Holly, Jerry Lee Lewis, Bill Haley and His Comets, and the Everly Brothers were some of the most significant white rock 'n' roll artists of the 1950s.

However, the most famous white star of early rock 'n' roll was Elvis Presley. Presley grew up in a poor, mostly Black neighborhood and attended Black churches. He was inspired by gospel music, such as that of Sister Rosetta Tharpe.

Much of Presley's early success came from covers of Black artists' songs. Later on, he sang more music that was written for him. Though there were major issues with white people using Black artists' music, Presley's work also had a positive effect.

More than 1 billion Elvis Presley records have sold worldwide. As of 2023, Guinness World Records recognizes him as the best-selling solo music artist of all time.

He helped make the genre popular and bring white and Black fans together. He acknowledged the Black artists who influenced him and opened some doors for Black musicians by opening white audiences' minds.

Presley's effects on rock 'n' roll weren't limited to drawing in more fans. He also added country-and-western elements to his music. This style was called rockabilly. It became a genre within rock 'n' roll in the years to come. Additionally, Presley was a young, handsome man with a suggestive style of singing and dancing. This made him popular among young audiences. He inspired teen trends. His influential career has inspired many to call him "the King of Rock 'n' Roll."

Elvis Presley died in 1977. In 2018, he was awarded the Presidential Medal of Freedom in honor of his contributions to American culture during his lifetime.

Teenage Tide

Teens' interest in rock 'n' roll played a big part in the genre's success. Though white adults often tried to prevent young people from listening to rock 'n' roll, teenagers loved the music. In part, they were drawn to it because it seemed rebellious. They liked listening to music their parents didn't approve of. They liked that the music referenced sex and race, topics that many adults considered inappropriate for teenagers.

The changing culture in the United States during the 1950s and 1960s helped set the stage for teens to become rock 'n' roll fans. Improvements in technology made it easier for teens to listen to the music. Radios and record players became smaller and more affordable. Teens could have them in their rooms. Radios were becoming more common in cars too. This meant that teenagers had much more freedom to listen to the music they wanted to, rather than

In the 1950s, electronics company Sharp made a portable radio for cars. It had strong magnets so it would stick to the dashboard.

The Arthur Murray Party was a TV show hosted by Arthur and Kathryn (*front center*) Murray. They were famous dancers at the time and used the show to advertise their dance studios.

what their parents liked. Radio stations created programs designed for teens. Many white teens began to turn their radios to the stations that targeted Black audiences, where they heard the R&B that would eventually evolve into rock 'n' roll.

Other aspects of American culture contributed to rock 'n' roll's rise. During the 1950s and 1960s, more families had enough money to buy luxuries. Teens had the spending money to buy records. They wanted to enjoy themselves and dance. In fact, many TV stations had dance shows where local teens could try new dance moves on camera. Sometimes Black and white teens would dance together in public, even when they were supposed to be segregated. Christian churches said that the popular dancing style was inappropriate and even associated it with the devil. But this just gave teens another rebellious reason to listen to the music.

THE DAY THE MUSIC DIED

Some people think the golden era of rock 'n' roll ended in the late 1950s. At that time, Little Richard quit playing rock 'n' roll, Elvis Presley was drafted into the US Army, and some other stars were in the middle of legal troubles or scandals. Then, on February 3, 1959, three rising stars of rock 'n' roll died in a plane crash. They were Ritchie Valens, Buddy Holly, and J. P. "the Big Bopper" Richardson. Their deaths symbolized the end of an era. Don McLean refers to that day as "the day the music died" in his 1971 song "American Pie."

Frankie Avalon became a popular singer as a teenager in the late 1950s and early 1960s. He also starred in several movies in the 1960s, becoming a teen idol.

Chapter 4

EVOLUTION AND REVOLUTION

The 1960s brought big changes to rock 'n' roll. Some people consider this era as a time when rock 'n' roll transitioned into rock. While rock 'n' roll was toned down at the start of the decade, the British Invasion brought the genre back with new twists. Meanwhile, American artists continued to innovate. The rebellious nature of rock 'n' roll soon returned as changes in American culture brought even more to rebel against.

The Evolution of American Rock

At the end of the 1950s and start of the 1960s, rock 'n' roll lost its rebellious reputation. Because parents worried about teenagers' love of rock 'n' roll, the music industry tried to tone it down. Record companies released records by clean-cut white singers. These included Frankie Avalon and Ricky Nelson. But the rebellious influences of rock 'n' roll couldn't be tamed for long.

Alongside these clean-cut crooners came new styles and sounds. The Beach Boys, Jan and Dean, and similar groups popularized the California sound. This was a style of rock 'n' roll music that often focused on an idealized vision of California life, full of carefree surfing and car cruising. Girl groups also began to make their marks in the male-dominated genre. Their music often combined sounds of gospel, R&B, doo-wop, and pop. Popular girl groups included the Shangri-Las, the Crystals, and the Ronettes.

Another key influence on rock 'n' roll in the 1960s and beyond was Motown. Motown was a record company based in Detroit, Michigan,

In the 1970s, Motown's headquarters moved to Los Angeles, California. The original location in Detroit is now a museum dedicated to Motown's history and legacy.

founded by Berry Gordy Jr. in 1958. Motown released hit after hit in its own unique style of soul music by Black artists. The Motown sound, as it was called, was designed to appeal to a wide variety of audiences. The Supremes, a girl group that debuted in 1964, were Motown's biggest success, but many Motown artists dominated the charts.

Young people had also started to listen to more folk music in the 1960s. Major folk artists such as Arlo Guthrie, Joan Baez, and Bob Dylan sang songs about many different subjects rather than just those that appealed to young teens. America's acoustic folk bands inspired skiffle bands in the United Kingdom. UK skiffle bands soon evolved into rock 'n' roll bands, setting the stage for the British Invasion.

Joan Baez (*left*) is a folk singer and songwriter. Many of her songs are about social justice. She helped Bob Dylan (*right*) become a popular singer and songwriter as well.

The British Invasion

Rock 'n' roll developed in the United States. But American rock 'n' roll music became popular overseas, especially in the United Kingdom. Many British music groups played American rock 'n' roll. The Beatles and other groups covered American rock 'n' roll classics. But they also wrote their own rock 'n' roll songs.

Beginning with the Beatles, rock 'n' roll music came to dominate the UK music charts. British songs soon topped the charts in America as well. The Beatles were quickly followed by the Rolling Stones, the Dave Clark Five, and many others. American teens loved British accents as

Many people credit the Rolling Stones with creating the sounds that came to define the hard rock genre during the early 1960s.

well as the new styles and slang that the groups popularized. But they also loved the music. Soon, British rock 'n' roll began to distinguish itself from its American roots, and fans loved it.

American bands such as the Monkees and the Byrds were heavily influenced by the Beatles, the Rolling Stones, and other British groups. Even established bands such as the Beach Boys were inspired by the music of British Invasion artists. With the British Invasion, rock 'n' roll came back in full force. Over time, the music evolved.

The Beach Boys started out as a garage band. They grew popular for their unique sound, which was a mix of old pop vocal sounds, rock 'n' roll, and R&B.

Rocking American Culture

During the 1960s, artists began to mix folk music with rock 'n' roll. At the 1965 Newport Folk Festival in Rhode Island, Bob Dylan added rock beats and electric guitar to his music, leading the folk-rock movement. Meanwhile, some rock 'n' roll groups played covers of folk songs, such as the Animals' 1964 version of "House of the Rising Sun."

Inspired by folk artists, many rock 'n' roll musicians started seeing themselves as artists rather than simply entertainers. Some bands focused on political issues in the United States and around the world. This new aspect of rock 'n' roll particularly appealed to college students.

In 1960s America, many people protested about political issues, hoping to change what they saw as problems in mainstream culture. These issues included civil rights, women's equality, the environment, and

In 2016, Bob Dylan received the Nobel Prize in Literature for his songwriting.

the controversial Vietnam War. These anti-establishment protests were referred to as the counterculture movement. Counterculture refers to a culture that is different from the norms of mainstream society.

The people in the counterculture movement were often inspired by rock 'n' roll songs. So, rock 'n' roll music became part of the counterculture. And over the course of the decade, it was also increasingly referred to as rock music. Rock and the counterculture constantly influenced each other. Drugs, sex, and rebellion were associated with 1960s counterculture. So were ideas of peace and love. Rock music lyrics often referenced these themes. The 1969 Woodstock music festival in Bethel, New York, became a major symbol of counterculture values.

In 1969, Beatles member John Lennon (*right*) married artist and musician Yoko Ono (*left*). Together, they formed a group called the Plastic Ono Band.

Black Music Evolves

While rock music evolved, another musical evolution was taking place. Although many white rock musicians and bands gained fame, few Black artists found the same success. Instead, many of them returned to R&B. They used the influence of rock music to develop R&B styles such as soul and funk.

But Black artists continued to influence rock music. Black women's gospel-inspired vocals were used in many rock recordings. Some Black musicians combined elements from many genres to innovate rock music. Well-known Black artists who did this included Jimi Hendrix and Sly and the Family Stone.

Music by Black artists had major influences on American culture. Motown music was prominent in the civil rights movement, helping to inspire people and bring them together. In 1967, R&B singer Aretha Franklin's song "Respect" became an anthem of the civil rights movement. Jimi Hendrix's guitar playing, use of technology, and rebellious stage presence changed rock music and rock culture forever.

Jimi Hendrix was the first musician to use guitar amplifier feedback as a sound effect in his songs.

In 1987, Aretha Franklin became the first female musician to be inducted into the Rock and Roll Hall of Fame.

British band Queen's first album came out in 1973, and the band is still popular today. Lead singer Freddy Mercury (*left*) died in 1991. Since then, Queen has had several different lead singers.

Chapter 5

WHAT'S NEXT?

Rock music grew and changed beyond the 1960s. Today, some people believe that rock music is dead. Other genres, particularly hip-hop and pop, have taken over as young people's preferred styles of music. In fact, hip-hop has dominated the US *Billboard* music charts since 2017. But rock artists still have more to say, and the legacy of rock 'n' roll lives on.

Rocking On

The 1960s brought huge changes to rock 'n' roll. Rock music continued to evolve in the coming decades. British bands continued to be very influential throughout the 1970s and 1980s, with a second British Invasion taking place in the 1980s. Different subgenres of rock developed, including glam, punk, alternative, grunge, and hard rock. Iconic rock bands emerged and developed strong fan bases. These bands included Queen, Bon Jovi, and Nirvana. Major rock stars of the era included Bruce Springsteen and David Bowie.

During this time, many Black musicians began turning to hip-hop and rap instead of rock. Hip-hop took inspiration from rock 'n' roll and other genres with Black roots. Like early rock 'n' roll, it was associated with rebellion. Additionally, pop music began to rise in popularity. As other genres topped the charts, the rock songs that did experience popular success were often considered pop rock. By the 2000s, pop and hip-hop were the dominant genres. Rock music's popularity faded.

Ruth Brown played a big role in the founding of the Rhythm and Blues Foundation in 1988. It is a nonprofit organization that works to preserve the history and culture of R&B music.

Women and Rock

Over the years, rock 'n' roll has been largely dominated by men. However, there have been some women who found success as rock musicians. Sister Rosetta Tharpe, Ruth Brown, and Memphis Minnie were a few of the women who had careers that inspired other artists and influenced rock 'n' roll itself. As the years went on, women began to have even more influence on rock. Girl groups such as the Shirelles, the Supremes, and the Ronettes recorded hit songs, and soon women rockers such as Tina Turner, Janis Joplin, Pat Benatar, and Joan Jett rose to fame. Punk rock also helped bring more women rockers to the forefront, including Siouxsie Sioux and Patti Smith.

Today, women continue to be essential voices in rock music. But women are still underrepresented. In 2019, only 7.7 percent of rockers in the Rock and Roll Hall of Fame were women. Women musicians struggle to have their music played on radio stations and promoted on music streaming platforms.

Joni Mitchell is one of the best-known artists to emerge from the 1960s. She has won ten Grammy Awards and is in the Rock and Roll Hall of Fame. Many consider her to be one of the greatest songwriters ever.

Is Rock 'n' Roll Dead?

Some people claim that rock 'n' roll is dead. The genre certainly isn't as popular as it once was. Top 40 radio, which is aimed at younger listeners, is filled with hip-hop and pop music. Rock music's popularity on streaming platforms has also dropped, particularly among younger listeners. Because of this, rock bands don't make as much money as hip-hop and pop artists do. This means they're not signed as often by record labels, so they have fewer opportunities to record their music.

Music technology has also played a role in rock's declining popularity. Digital production technology allows producers to create many effects. The effects can imitate the sound of instruments without using a full band. Popular music today emphasizes digital production effects, but these effects generally aren't used in rock music.

Music streaming services such as Spotify make it possible for listeners to explore all genres of music.

Changes in American culture are another factor in rock 'n' roll's decline. Today, few people consider rock music to be immoral, so teenagers aren't drawn to it as an act of rebellion. Young people today are surrounded by technology and social media. This may influence their tastes, creating an interest in more digitally produced music and performances with visual effects. Young people are also exposed to more marketing and advertising from record companies promoting pop and hip-hop songs.

But this doesn't mean that rock 'n' roll is dead. There are still musicians creating rock music and seeing high turnouts at their concerts. These artists continue to innovate and write music that speaks to younger audiences. Young musicians cover rock 'n' roll classics and blend them with new styles. And platforms such as TikTok allow people to share their music. Musicians no longer need contracts with record companies for their music to be heard.

Modern computer technology helps musicians and music producers create and change sounds digitally. This includes changing the sound of a singer's voice by adding special effects.

An American Legacy

Rock 'n' roll changed America. It had a huge influence on American music and music worldwide. Its influence can still be heard in today's popular music. And rock 'n' roll's influence reached beyond music. It has impacted American culture. Today, people see classic rock 'n' roll as a symbol of America. Americans as a whole still rank rock as their favorite genre, even though people consume more hip-hop and pop overall.

Rock 'n' roll stood for many different values. It helped bring about major changes in American society, such as improved racial equality. While the future of rock music is unclear, American rock artists aren't going to stop making music anytime soon. No matter what the future holds, rock 'n' roll will continue to influence American music—and America—for generations to come.

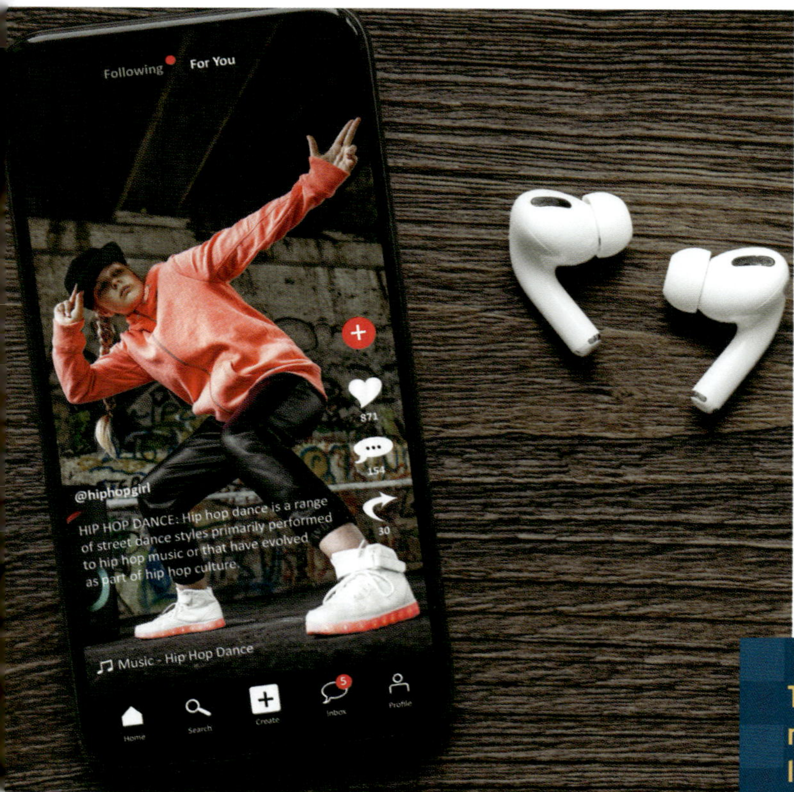

TikTok has become a promotional tool for many in the music industry. Musicians looking to make their music popular will reach out to influencers to share their songs and gain a larger audience.

Rock 'n' roll music still influences many artists. Bruno Mars (*left*) is a popular contemporary singer. He said he has been inspired by early rock 'n' roll stars including Little Richard and Jimi Hendrix.

MAKE AMERICANA!

What can you create that is inspired by rock 'n' roll? Start by thinking about your favorite rock 'n' roll songs, artists, and historical themes. Then put your imagination to work!

Paint old CDs black. Glue on patterned paper and letters cut out of magazines. Use the CDs to **decorate your room** or as **gifts for your music-loving friends**!

Cut a square out of an old T-shirt to **make a rock 'n' roll themed patch**! Paint words and designs with bleach. Decorate it with metal brads. Then use safety pins to attach it to a jacket or backpack.

Turn old fuzzy socks into fingerless gloves to wear at a concert! Cut off the toes and cut a hole near the end of each sock for your thumbs. Then sew on strips cut from an old T-shirt and other decorations.

TIMELINE

1922
The term *rock and roll* is used in the song "My Baby Rocks Me with One Steady Roll" by Trixie Smith.

APRIL 1951
"Rocket 88" is released, credited to Jackie Brenston and His Delta Cats. It is widely considered to be the first rock 'n' roll song.

JULY 1951
DJ Alan Freed starts his R&B radio show, where he popularizes the term rock 'n' roll.

JANUARY 1959
Berry Gordy Jr. founds a record label in Detroit, Michigan. It would go on to become Motown Records.

FEBRUARY 1959
A plane crash kills three rising stars of rock 'n' roll: Buddy Holly, Ritchie Valens, and J. P. "the Big Bopper" Richardson. The crash symbolizes the end of a golden era of rock 'n' roll.

1964

The Beatles perform on *The Ed Sullivan Show*, making their American television debut. This marks the beginning of the British Invasion.

1967

Aretha Franklin's song "Respect" becomes an anthem of the civil rights movement.

1965

Bob Dylan plays an electric guitar when he performs at the Newport Folk Festival, mixing folk music and rock 'n' roll.

1969

The Woodstock music festival takes place, featuring rock 'n' roll and folk-rock artists. It becomes a symbol of the 1960s counterculture and rock's influence on it.

1980s

A second British Invasion occurs.

2017

Hip-hop overtakes rock as the most popular genre in the United States.

GLOSSARY

a cappella–without accompanying instrumental music.

acoustic–music created using instruments whose sound is not dependent on electrical equipment.

captivate–to influence or fascinate by some special charm.

debut–a first appearance or to make a first appearance.

draft–to select for required military service.

forefront–the most important part or position.

genre–a type of art, music, or literature.

immoral–not following certain principles of right and wrong.

innovate–to introduce something new or do something in a new way. A new product or method is an innovation.

legacy–something important or meaningful handed down from previous generations or from the past.

lyrics–the words of a song.

rebellion–open opposition to authority. Something related to a rebellion is rebellious.

segregation–the separation of an individual or a group from a larger group, especially by race.

suggestive—causing thoughts that are sexual in nature.

tempo—how fast a song is played or sung.

transition—to move or change from one state, stage, or style to another.

ONLINE RESOURCES

Booklinks
NONFICTION NETWORK
FREE! ONLINE NONFICTION RESOURCES

To learn more about rock 'n' roll, please visit **abdobooklinks.com** or scan this QR code. These links are routinely monitored and updated to provide the most current information available.

INDEX